Reader's Guides

SECOND SERIES 2

FISHING

by

ARTHUR RANSOME

C.B.E., Litt.D.

T0345967

PUBLISHED FOR

THE NATIONAL BOOK LEAGUE

AT THE UNIVERSITY PRESS

CAMBRIDGE

1955

CAMBRIDGE UNIVERSITY PRESS
Cambridge, New York, Melbourne, Madrid, Cape Town,
Singapore, São Paulo, Delhi, Mexico City

Cambridge University Press
The Edinburgh Building, Cambridge CB2 8RU, UK

Published in the United States of America by Cambridge University Press, New York

www.cambridge.org
Information on this title: www.cambridge.org/9781107622180

First published 1955
Re-issued 2013

A catalogue record for this publication is available from the British Library

ISBN 978-1-107-62218-0 Paperback

Contents

Introduction

THE Very Reverend Patrick Murray Smythe, who was born in 1860, kept a fishing diary from March 1872, when he recorded the capture of sixteen sticklebacks and a minnow ("I ate minnow"), to March 1935, his last entry being made only a few days before his death. In this delightful book, which has been edited by his son and is shortly to be published, he mentions a day on Loch Leven with "old Mr. Butters who spends his summers in fishing and his winters in thinking about it". But that is what most fishermen do in winter when the clogging frivolities of business allow them freedom for their minds. Thinking about fishing in winter . . . the fisherman's body may be sitting at a table in a lamp-lit room but he is far away, listening to the splash and tumble at the weir, noting the dimple of a trout on a smooth run between the weed-beds, feeling his heart quicken at the stir of a salmon not leaping into the air but rising modestly and quietly, sure sign of a taking fish, or maybe watching his float, long idle by the waterlilies, twitch suddenly to life. Thinking about fishing in winter . . . what is it but "the spontaneous overflow of powerful feelings; it takes its origin from emotion recollected in tranquillity". But that is Wordsworth's definition of poetry. What wonder is it that more good books have been written about fishing than about any other sport? What wonder that fishermen, when they cannot fish, enjoy reading those good books?

In fishing books instruction and reminiscence are inextricably plaited together. Even the books that purport to tell a simple story contrive to make or find themselves making pupils of their readers. And many of the books that set out merely to be instructive are lit by the glow of recollected emotion and turn to poetry without knowing it. This perhaps in part explains why there are so many estimable men who, pending their transfer to a well-watered heaven, buy every fishing book as soon as it is published. They admit that some fishing books are not very good. What they claim is that they can take pleasure even in a bad book, so long as it is about fishing. They enjoy agreeing with one man and enjoy disagreeing with another and in both may find that same authentic glow of poetry, without suspecting, generous fellows, that, in some cases, they may have put it there themselves.

The pedagogic instinct is widely spread among men. No sooner has man learnt a new trick than he looks for a pupil to whom to teach it. There are men who when they learn a very old trick are inclined to write a book about it and to believe that it is a discovery of their own. This instinct is the excuse for many books about fishing, but not the reason why so many of them are good. The teachers call upon their own experience to illustrate their lessons, and, once they do that, the emotions of the past come rushing back and all is incandescent. Now of all stimulants to the pedagogic instinct among fishermen the most successful is the discovery of some new method or of some new material that brings about the modification of an old. Men try it, catch fish with it, and buy a ream of paper and a fountain pen. A good example is the spate of books produced not by the modest inventor of the fixed spool reel but by others excited at finding what they could do with it. The invention of nylon casts and lines has loosed a flood of ink. But nothing has so stimulated the production of fishing books as the continual production of new flies. All fishing other than mere netting, snaring or base assault with spear or arrow, consists in deluding the fish into taking a natural or

6

artificial bait. But whereas there is no end to the permutations and combinations of feathers and silk and hair there are narrow limits to the changes that can be rung on natural baits. It has been established once for all that gilt-tails are the worms for grayling, and lobs the best for most other fishes, though brandlings are preferred by some. Sheringham has written delightfully of lob-hunting with a torch after dark on a dew-moistened lawn. I have heard a party of match-fishers in a railway carriage arguing over the tinting of maggots, praising this one chrysoidine, that one anatta, and seen them, each to prove his point, set their big fatted gentles, in gorgeous colours, wriggling on the table between them. Cheese, plums, potatoes, brewer's grains, caddis-worms, macaroni, bread-crust, paste, hempseed, stewed wheat . . . it is possible to make a long list of natural baits but it is very short in comparison with the ever-lengthening roll call of artificial flies. Natural baits do not make a very deep demand on the imagination or observation of the angler. As a subject for argument they may serve for a railway journey, but not from one year's end to another. They give the fisherman less to talk about, less to write about. Yet, though the coarse fishermen do not so naturally and so continually run to ink, we owe them some of the very best of our books, beginning with Izaak Walton. The very simplicity, the comparative uniformity of his preparations leaves the float-fisher free to relish ecstatic immobility at the waterside, where the fly-fisher, creeping and crawling and keeping his balance, cannot in the same way surrender himself to the moment. The float-fishers produce fewer books, but among them are the best. I think of the chapters on fishing, chapters from which the very essence of angling pleasure seems to distil like the mist rising on a summer's morning from a placid river, that were written by a Russian, Sergei Aksakov (1791—1859), who said that trout-fishing was "too restless" and preferred to watch his float. No

7

man has written as well as he of the ecstasy felt by a boy as he comes to the river and of the calm happiness felt by an old man fishing in the evening of his life the waters he knew as a boy.

All the same, I cannot imagine anybody writing a whole book about maggots, whereas many a man has spent much of his life in thinking and writing about the fisherman's flies. And how well some of these observers write, hurrying from the riverside to the fly-tying bench and then back to the river to have another look at the models they are trying to imitate with silk and feather. At the beginning was the revered Juliana with her dozen flies. And today there are men so interested in this kind of portraiture that they have little time to spare for fishing. J. W. Dunne, the philosopher, profited like Newton from a happy accident. He tied some flies with artificial silk and noticed that their bodies turned black. He then tied them on white-painted hooks and, oiling them before showing them to a fish, perceived that they became miraculously translucent. His flies are rather bothersome to tie, though one or two of them, notably his Black Gnats, are very rewarding, but his account of how he came to tie them as he did is such that nobody who has read his book would care afterwards to be without it, no matter what flies he himself may put on his cast. Listen to this, of the final descent of the "orange quills": "It was over in the twinkling of an eye. They appeared, a small cloud, flying swiftly from the shadows of a group of branching trees. For one instant they sparkled, flaming red, in the sunlight—and then they had gone to the water like a rush of little fireworks, and were extinguished by the rising trout." Those sentences are good observation, good natural history, and, touched by emotion recollected in tranquillity, are they not also close akin to poetry?

Writing is a form of living. Readers, overhearing as it were an author muttering to himself, share his experience in so far as they are capable, but, being different from him, modify it into an experience of their own. It is obvious that reader and author share in a book's success and that the character of that success depends on both of them. For that reason it is waste of time to try to make a list of the best dozen or even the best hundred books on fishing and to try to impose that list on others. The best hundred for me would not be the best hundred for somebody else, and even if they were he would arrange them in a different order. Further, read by him, they would each one of them be different from the same books read by me or by anybody else whomsoever. Yet, next to the pleasure of reading a favourite fishing book comes that of persuading a friend to read it too. Many is the book that I have lost by foolishly pressing a friend, whom I wished to convert, to borrow it and to take it away in his pocket. We are, all of us, inveterate propagandists. When the National Book League invited me to glance over the whole field of English books on fishing I at first rejoiced in what I thought would be the easy task of helping such a young man as once I was to choose the books that should form the nucleus of his fishing library, but presently despaired, remembering the great variety of young men and the incredible number of fishing books among which they have to choose. Once upon a time it would have been easy because there were but a handful of books on fishing. Since then the books have seeded and multiplied until what was once a mere grove has turned into a forest through which a newcomer may find it hard to pick his way. Where should he begin?

I propose to give no advice, but instead, to look along my own shelves and give a free rein to favouritism. Which are the books to which most often I return? I will not in that short list include the reference books that go with me on a fishing holiday, to be consulted perhaps half a dozen times a day. Yet some of these are good books in their own right. Even if they were not, I should still, having a bad memory, want them with me. But they go on the permanent list of fishing gear, not to be forgotten, thus: "Rods, reels, casts, flies, net, gaff, wading staff, waders, brogues, waterproof jacket and Colonel Maunsell." Most so-called "Vade Mecums" are best left at home, but not so his (published by Philip Allan in 1933) and, thanks to the enormous improvement in nylon casts and lines and the slipperiness of nylon, which has made us all as interested as sailors in the tying of knots, Colonel Maunsell must be joined by Dr. Barnes whose *Anglers' Knots in Gut and Nylon* (Cornish Bros.) solves all nodal difficulties, trains the clumsiest fingers and provides delightful entertainment for those hours (which occur even on a fishing holiday) when fishing would be a waste of time. Still, we do not read those books for their own sake. We turn their pages perhaps desperately with an urgent ulterior motive (because time, tide and rising fish wait for no man). Let me mention here a few books to be read for the simple pleasure of reading them and not with a view to the immediate acquiring of some technical skill, although, so important is the spirit in which we fish, that a book that puts us in the mood to enjoy our fishing is likely also by some happy miracle to put us in the way of catching more or bigger fish.

First of all must come Izaak Walton, who "studied to be quiet" in times almost as troubled as our own. I have him in several editions but I am sure that anyone who does not already know him should make a point of meeting him first in the World's Classics where is John Buchan's admirable introduction to Walton and Cotton together. There are plenty of other editions, but John Buchan makes this my favourite, though I should be sorry to be without the charming brown-leather-jerkined facsimile of the first edition of *The Compleat Angler* published (a noble act of piety) by A. and C. Black, to whom fishermen owe so much. Here it is, the little brown dumpling of a book just as it slipped modestly into existence, in St. Dunstan's churchyard in Fleet Street in 1653, that critical, stirring year of the Commonwealth, four years after Charles the First had been beheaded, the year of the dissolution of the Long Parliament, six years before the Restoration, and yet a year when Piscator could stretch his legs up Totnam Hill to go fishing by Ware "this fine pleasant fresh May day in the morning".

Here is another first edition, and no facsimile this time but the real thing, the actual first edition of Robert Nobbes's *The Compleat Troller*, "printed by T. James for Tho. Helder at the Angel in Little Britain" in 1682, a book on pike-fishing, the first of the many specialist books to be written by men devoted to one particular fish. That is a rare book, but here is one still rarer. It is "Arundo's" own copy of Robert Salter's *The Modern Angler*, printed at Oswestry and inter-leaved with paper on which "Arundo", John Beever of the Thwaite, Coniston, wrote the notes that were turned at last into his own *Practical Fly-fishing founded on nature*. John Beever's book was first published in 1849. The son of a Manchester merchant, who, on retirement, moved first to the banks of the Dove and then to Coniston, he was a brother of Miss Susanna Beever, the botanist who established a drinking fountain for horses on the steep hill up to High Cross, on which a grateful driver scratched the words "God bless Miss Beever!" He was an alert, observant fisherman. Long before Stewart he urged his pupils to "get below their fish, or, at any rate abreast of them". He makes critical notes on Salter's flies, and, tucked into his copy of Salter is an admirable ink drawing of "middle duns" drawn from life in April 1818. On another page he has written indignantly, "Mr. William Beever of Birdsgrove on the Dove (his father) has in attempting to stain red hackles sullied this part of my book. I hope his red was more brilliant than the stains indicate". His ghost, and

11

perhaps his father's also, would be amused to observe that the stains have faded out of existence. He tells of a fisherman who taught him much, the Matlock coach-driver who, when some young men called his attention to some fish they had not been able to catch, caught them all one after another and looked up from the river to ask, "And now, gentlemen, can you show me any more?" That little scene is played before our eyes and a hundred years are gone as if by magic. At the same time, John Beever dates himself most accurately in the period when the stage coach was yielding to the railway. He complained that ferruled rods in short joints were made not for fishing but for portability. "When we had only small coaches to squeeze ourselves and our rods into, there was an excuse for this; but as travelling is now chiefly performed by steam . . . a few feet in the length of a parcel is no objection, either upon the roof of a railway carriage or the deck of a steamer."

I was doubtful about mentioning my dear John Beever, because like Salter, he is out of print. But why deprive a collector of the pleasures of the chase? After all, fishermen value most the fish that are hard to take and value least those that are offered to everybody on a fishmonger's slab. The young fisherman putting together a library for himself should by no means neglect the secondhand bookshops. But he will not always prefer a first edition to a later one. I prize an old edition of *Fly-fishing* by Sir Edward Grey, but I should hate to be without *Fly-fishing* by Viscount Grey of Fallodon, published thirty years later and enriched by the new chapters, "Spring Salmon Fishing—the Cassley" and "Retrospect", which I read and re-read, though never without turning back to his description of leaving London by Waterloo at about six o'clock in a summer morning on the way to Test or Itchen. "There are places where hansoms can be found even at these hours of the morning; they are not numerous, and they seem quite different from the hansoms that are abroad at more lively hours, but they can be found if you will look for them at certain places." Like difficult fish or books out of print.

Then, going back a little earlier, there is Thomas Tod Stoddart's *Angler's Companion to the rivers and lochs of Scotland*, and his entertaining *Reminiscences* with the account of a day's fishing with the Ettrick Shepherd. And, most lovable of all books on Tweedside fishing, there is *River Angling for Salmon and Trout* by John Younger the shoemaker of St. Boswell's, who, proudly apologising for his style, said it was "the very best style the author can possibly afford from thirty shillings' worth of scholastic education". He was born in 1785, and, over a hundred years ago, suggested that when trout were feeding below the surface the angler should tie down the wings of his flies to near the tail, to give them an appearance "something like the maggot released from its first case on the bottom stone and on its ascent to the surface" and "as much as you can, let them sink low in the water", an early foreshadowing of the present-day tying and fishing of nymphs.

Then here is an 1857 edition of W. C. Stewart's *The Practical Angler* of which J. W. Hills, who wrote good books himself, said "Surely still of its kind the best book ever written". Stewart, like Younger, urged upstream fishing for trout, whereas Cholmondeley Pennell in *The Modern Practical Angler* pooh-poohed it, perhaps from that same contrariness that made him declare that imitation of nature was needless and that three flies, red, green and yellow, were enough. Here they both are and also the little pamphlet *Caution to Anglers*, a pamphlet of embittered argument between the two of them in which there are accusations of plagiary, of lying and even of bad fishing. Well, they have both long been dead and, I suppose, fish the Styx, one fishing up and one fishing down and pass each other without speaking. Stewart's is the better book and the better advice but Pennell's is also worth reading.

13

Here is my father's copy of Pritt's *Yorkshire Trout Flies*, (1886) and in it an old hair cast with a "light partridge and yellow" still surviving. I remember as a small boy taking feathers from birds my father had shot to Pritt lying ill in bed. Pritt gives sixty two patterns, but my father's copy has a manuscript note, "An old fellow in Upper Wharfedale used following casts. (1) Little Black and Yellow, Waterhen, Woodcock, Snipe and purple till April 26 (i.e. arrival of swallows) when he changed to (2) March Brown, Iron Blue Dun, Light Snipe and Yellow Partridge, which he fished through the season and always did as well as anyone. T. E. Pritt". Then here is *Wet Fly-fishing* by E. M. Tod (another old friend of my family) with a picture of Mr. Tod himself landing a trout while using his ingenious dodge for slinging his net on his basket. Honest old man! He had to explain in a footnote that the "trout" being landed was no trout but a mackerel bought for the purpose. And here is the book of another friend long dead, *Fishing in Eden* by William Nelson of Appleby who when someone said that the Eden needed restocking went out to prove it did not, and came back with a basket of over sixty trout. His is a well loved and memorable book with its picture of long ago boyhood in the Eden valley, and the cobbler, old Bob, who taught the lads how to tie their flies and how to use them. Another old favourite is Stephen Oliver (*Scenes and Recollections of Flyfishing*, 1834) who over a hundred years ago knew well that books and fishing go together, travelling light through the Lake District, always with a volume of Wordsworth, sending the other volumes on ahead of him with a change of underlinen.

But I am rattling on too long. That is the trouble with a fisherman among his books. You have but to start him talking and he goes rattling on for ever. And I have said nothing of H.T. Sheringham, " Piscator Rotundus", "The All-round Fisherman", as he used smilingly to explain. His is a row of delightful books with his *Coarse Fishing* perhaps the best of all. And that reminds me of J. W. Martin, the fishing tackle maker, in whose shop Sheringham loved to linger. Martin's *Coarse Fish Angling* is a fit companion to Sheringham's. He was an admirable writer, and, like the shoemaker of St. Boswell's, has his proud apology; "This is not a literary production; my schooldays were few and my buffets in the world many, but it is a plain unvarnished tale of my own personal experiences." And still there are many books not yet mentioned that never gather dust. What about Hamish Stuart's *Book of the Sea Trout*, all eager argument and infectious pleasure? What about Chaytor's *Letters to a Salmon Fisher's Sons*? What of Francis Francis, Scrope, the dogmatic Kelson who attributed to salmon a very discriminating taste in feathers, and in our own day, J. W. Hills, Ian Chalmers, Anthony Bridges, G. E. M. Skues, Dr. Turrell and half a hundred others? I must stop taking books from the shelves. After all, I have got to put them back again.

One thing has become clear, at least to me, as I have been taking down one book after another. Fishing books, lit by emotion recollected in tranquillity, are like poetry in more than that. When we think of poetry, we think of poets. "And did you once see Shelley plain?" It was of Shelley Browning was thinking, of Shelley the man and not of some particular edition of his *Works*. So it is with our fishing books. We do not think of them as books but as men. They are our companions and not only at the riverside. Summer and winter they are with us and what a pleasant company they are. All trades are represented here. Here is Walton the ironmonger and friend of bishops, Cotton the somewhat graceless cavalier, Plunket-Greene the singer, Younger the cobbler, Martin and Walbran who kept fishing tackle shops, Nelson the schoolmaster, Grey the politician, sundry journalists, many soldiers, a bench of lawyers, a synod of parsons, and Thomas

Tod Stoddart who, when a contemporary who had risen high in the world asked him what he was doing, replied almost with indignation, "Doing? Doing? Man, I'm an Angler".

The Fisherman's Library

The output of new books on fishing is now so large that not even the greediest and most omnivorous of readers can pretend to know them all. The following list, of time-tested old books and recommended new ones, includes the suggestions of a number of readers. Omission from it does not imply criticism of the book omitted. In each section books published before 1900 are grouped at the beginning, divided by a rule. All publishers are London firms, except where otherwise stated. So far as possible dates of the latest editions are given. Prices (net and subject to alteration) are given only where a book is known to be available new at the time this pamphlet goes to press.

THE INDISPENSABLES

Where to Fish. 1955–1956 (Ed. Roy C. Eaton) The Field, Harmsworth Press. 66th edition, 1954. 21s.

There can be no fishing if we do not know where to fish, and this book is a detailed guide to the fishing obtainable in England, Wales, Scotland and Ireland with useful notes on fishing in Africa, Australia, Canada and Europe. This is its 66th edition. It has grown from small beginnings, and now includes a folding map of the fishing rivers of Great Britain, as well as detailed information about free fishing and the cost of tickets for fishing where available. Few fishing holidays for the last fifty years can have been planned without its help.

BARNES, STANLEY. *Anglers' Knots in Gut and Nylon.* Birmingham, Cornish, revised edition 1951, 18s.

The late Dr. Barnes, formerly Dean of the Faculty of Medicine, University of Birmingham, put all fishermen (including many yet unborn) in his debt by devoting much of his leisure on retirement to the scientific testing of known knots and the devising of new ones in the materials most likely to be used either in float-fishing, spinning, or fly-fishing.

MAUNSELL, G. W. *The Fisherman's Vade Mecum*. Allan, 1933. 3rd edition, Black, 1952. 18s.

On a fishing expedition this must not be left behind.

VENABLES, BERNARD. *Guide to Angling Waters*. Daily Mirror, 12s. 6d.

Another helpful guide of a more specialized character than *Where to Fish*, discussing the rivers and still waters of a general defined South East, including the Thames, the Great Ouse and the Suffolk rivers, the Hampshire Avon and the waters of Sussex and Kent, with excellent sectional maps and some delightful illustrations.

TROUT FISHING

CLAPHAM, RICHARD. *Trout Fishing on Hill Streams*. Edinburgh, Oliver & Boyd, 1947. 3s. 6d.

Mr. Clapham, fishing north county becks, is "practically" a one-fly man. "For a good many years I have used no other pattern of fly but the Black Spinner, otherwise Lee's Favourite." "He has no objection to other flies, provided that they are lightly dressed, but he does extremely well without them."

EDYE, HUISH. *The Angler and the Trout*. Black, 1945. 10s. 6d.

Instructive and amusing. Mainly chalk-stream fishing. "A season does not pass in which I do not find myself misguided by following one of my favourite precepts." That is the remark of a man from whom it is a pleasure to learn.

GREENE, H. PLUNKET. *Where the Bright Waters Meet*. Allan, 1924.

One of the best-loved books of reminiscence.

HILLS, J. W. *A Summer on the Test*. Allan, 1930; Bles, 1946. 12s. 6d.

This book by one who grew up on the Eden conveys the very essence of chalk-stream fishing.

IVENS, T. C. *Still Water Fly-fishing*. Verschoyle, 1952 (Deutsch). 16s.

On reservoir fishing, mainly with wet fly.

LAWRIE, W. H. *The Book of the Rough Stream Nymph*. Edinburgh, Oliver & Boyd, 1947. 6s.

A sensible little book discussing the right application of Mr.

Skues's practice and theory (see below) in the different conditions that obtain in our impatient northern streams.

MORRITT, H. E. *Fishing Ways and Wiles*. Cape, 2nd edition. 1950. 10s. 6d.

An entirely charming book, mainly on trout-fishing but with admirable chapters on sea-trout and salmon. No fisherman could read it without increasing both his enjoyment of fishing and his skill.

MOSS, H. W. *The Elements of Fly Fishing for Trout and Grayling*. Faber, 1951. 9s. 6d.

The beginner will find here all he needs besides reference to the books that will help him when he is a beginner no more.

POWELL, T. A. *Here and There a Lusty Trout*. Faber, 1947.

A book of ripe experience (mostly on the Kentish Stour) giving detailed dressings of some "tried and trusty deceivers".

ROLLO, W. KEITH. *Fly Fishing*. Witherby (Sports and Pastimes Library), 1931. 9s. 6d.

Particularly good on the Eden and other northern rivers.

SKUES, G. E. M. *Itchen Memories*. Herbert Jenkins, 1951. 12s. 6d.

This is a posthumous book of notes, memories and suggestions by the great pioneer of nymph-fishing. Like all the great pioneers, he was never willing to let well alone but was always prepared to go one better. This book gives his final commentary on the views expressed in earlier books:—*Minor Tactics of the Chalk Stream*. Black, 1910. 3rd edition, 1950. 16s.; *The Way of a Trout with a Fly*. Black, 1921. 4th edition 1949. 16s.; *Sidelines, Side-lights and Reflections*. Seeley Service, 1932.

TAVERNER, ERIC. *Trout Fishing from all Angles*. Seeley Service, 1929. 25s.

Encyclopaedic.

TOD, E. M. *Wet Fly Fishing*. Fishing Gazette.

A hardy perennial.

WALKER, C. F. *Riverside Reflections*. Edinburgh, Oliver & Boyd, 1952. 10s. 6d.

Delightfully written essays and memories by the author of *Chalk Stream Flies*.

GRAYLING

PLATTS, W. CARTER. *Grayling Fishing*. Black, 1939.
Encyclopaedic.

PRITT, T. E. *The Book of the Grayling*. 1888.

ROLT, H. A. *Grayling Fishing in South Country Streams*. Sampson Low, 1905.

WALBRAN, F. M. *Grayling and How to Catch Them*, 1895.

SEA-TROUT FISHING

BRIDGETT, R. C. *Sea-Trout Fishing*. Herbert Jenkins, 1929.

Two books in one. The first talks of tackle and how to use it. The second is made up of memories of fishing, alike delightful and instructive.

BLUETT, JEFFERY. *Sea Trout and Occasional Salmon*. Cassell, 1948.

Mr. Bluett "most strongly recommends the beginner to read all he can" and goes on to say that of all books on angling first and foremost he places Hamish Stuart. He fishes mostly in the West Country, and mostly at night. His directions for night-time fishing are the most detailed and the most explanatory that have been published, and he urges the beginner to specialize at first in one type of river and one branch of fishing. A most likeable book.

CHRYSTAL, MAJOR R. A. *Angling Theories and Methods*. Herbert Jenkins, 1927.

Writes with the utmost respect of Hamish Stuart. Major Chrystal fished the Hebridean waters that Hamish Stuart knew and his book is a valuable commentary on Stuart besides discussing other sea-trout waters, loch-fishing generally, salmon, short rising and much else.

CLAPHAM, RICHARD. *Fishing for Sea-Trout in Tidal Water*. Edinburgh, Oliver & Boyd, 1950. 7s. 6d.

Mainly spinning with fixed spool reel in the tidal waters of rivers running into Morecambe Bay. His favourite spinner is a natural minnow in a celluloid jacket. He gives precise directions for using it.

HENZELL, H. P. *Fishing for Sea-Trout*. Black, 1949. 16s.

Practical instruction by one who is prepared to spin but prefers fly-fishing and with almost lyrical praise gives the Black Pennell its due. Mr. Henzell uses it dry as well as wet and also for dapping. He urges that for the good of the fishing anglers should restrict themselves in the taking of immature sea trout (herling or finnock). He gives detailed advice about fishing Loch Maree and other lochs, including those made famous by Hamish Stuart.

MOTTRAM, J. C. *Sea Trout and other Fishing Studies*. The Field, 1925.

A thoughtful, stimulating book by an original thinker.

STUART, HAMISH. *The Book of the Sea Trout*. 1st edition, 1917; 2nd edition, Cape, 1952. 16s.

This book of "controversial theory, practical wisdom and infectious pleasure" was unfinished when its author died at sea on a voyage undertaken in the hope of recovering his health. It was edited by his friend, Rafael Sabatini, himself a fine fisher and a magnificent fly-dresser, and published in a small edition in 1917. Stuart was a most successful fisherman. He was equally successful in starting discussion, and very little has been written on sea trout since his day that has not had something to say of his theories and methods.

SALMON

BALFOUR-KINNEAR, G. P. R. *Flying Salmon*. 2nd edition, Black, 1947. 15s.

The original edition of this book was published by Longmans, Green in 1937 and reprinted the next year. I mention this because for some reason unexplained the author has omitted from this new and enlarged edition his original, instructive and very entertaining chapter on fishing with a hookless fly. Those who, like me, want to re-read that chapter must do some careful fishing in the secondhand bookshops. The author may have had good reason for changing his mind about the hookless droppers, but he has not told us what it was. No matter. Even without that missing chapter, his is a valuable and most amusing book.

BRIDGES, ANTHONY. *Modern Salmon Fishing*. Black, 1947. 16s.

An instructive book by a very tolerant fisherman who thinks that "for sheer fascination" spinning for salmon with a thread-line outfit, "is comparable only to dry-fly fishing". Others who dislike organ-grinding do not agree with him. But his is a good book.

CHALMERS, IAN. *Salmon Fishing in Little Rivers*. Black, 1938.

A charming, modest book about salmon fishing of the less expensive sort, the fishing that most of us enjoy, ghillie-less, carefree fishing with a rod that can be used single-handed. Mr. Chalmers urges the salmon fisher in small rivers to confine himself to fly-fishing "because it is my firmest conviction that the fly accounts for far more fish from this type of river than any other lure".

CHAYTOR, A. H. *Letters to a Salmon Fisher's Son*. Murray, 1910. New edition, 1936. 12s. 6d.

At every new reading, the fisherman will find himself learning something he had missed before.

CROSSLEY, ANTHONY. *The Floating Line for Salmon and Sea-Trout*. With a chapter on the dry fly for salmon, by John Rennie, a number of letters between A. H. E. Wood and other fishermen and a commentary by W. J. Barry. 3rd edition, 1948. Methuen, 6s.

This extremely alert account of Wood's methods is by far the best that has so far appeared and one that historians will find invaluable.

GILBERT, H. A. *The Tale of a Wye Fisherman*. 2nd edition, Cape, 1953. 16s.

This account of fishing in the Wye, illustrated by excellent photographs of the river, is also a new edition. It has been greatly enriched by a chapter on the methods of Robert Pashley, who has fished the Wye since 1906 and in one year, using for the most part a trout rod and small flies, killed 678 salmon.

SCOTT, JOCK. *Greased Line Fishing for Salmon*. Seeley Service, 5th edition, 1950. 16s.

Compiled from the papers of A. H. E. Wood. With contributions from some of his friends, pictures of his flies and diagrams showing his methods.

TAVERNER, ERIC. *Salmon Fishing*. Seeley Service (The Lonsdale Library), 1948. 30s.

A useful compendium that includes the book on salmon flies mentioned among other books on fly-dressing.

TAVERNER, ERIC and BROWNE, W. BARRINGTON. *The Running of the Salmon*. Bles, 15s.

A well-told story of the salmon cycle, beginning with the fish leaving the feeding grounds, working towards the coast, the estuary and the river, past dangers of porpoises, seals, and fishermen and up to the spawning beds, death after death on the way, until the rare survivors, facing new risks, go seaward again, while eggs hatch, alevins turn to parr and parr to smolts until the "first flood in May sweeps smolts away" to the rich feeding of the sea and the cycle begins anew. Illustrated in colour and monochrome.

WADDINGTON, RICHARD. *Salmon Fishing, a new Philosophy*. Peter Davies, 1947. 16s.

Fly Fishing for Salmon. A modern Technique. Faber, 1951. 16s. Two argumentative books by the inventor of jointed hooks, the main fly being tied on a straight wire and the rest of it on a small triangle attached to it by a flexible joint. These hooks are said to be very good holders.

COARSE FISHING

BAZLEY, J. H. R. and WEATHERALL, M. *Coarse Fishing*. Witherby, 1932. 2nd edition (Sports and Pastimes Library) 1954. 9s. 6d.

An alert and lively book by an observant float-fisher, a Leeds schoolmaster who was twice the individual winner of the All-England championship.

"BB". *Confessions of a Carp-Fisher*. Eyre & Spottiswoode, 1950. 9s.

Accounts of carp-fishing by the author, by Richard Walker and by other captors of very large specimens. ("BB" is the editor of *The Fisherman's Bedside Book*, an admirable anthology published by the same firm.)

Fine Angling for Coarse Fish. By several authors. Edited by Eric Parker. Seeley Service (Lonsdale Library), 1947. 21s.

Encyclopaedic.

"How to Catch Them" series, edited by Kenneth Mansfield. Herbert Jenkins. 1954. 3s. 6d. each.

Tench by Harry Bretherton, *Roach* by Capt. L. A. Parker, *Bream* by Peter Tombleson, *Perch* by Kenneth Mansfield, *Chub* by Michael Shephard, *Pike* by A. L. Ward, *Bass* by Alan Young, *Trout* by W. A. Adamson. (Practical monographs by specialists.)

MARTIN, J. W. *Coarse Fish Angling, Days Among the Pike and Perch, My Fishing Days and Fishing Ways.*

Three admirable books first published early in this century and later reissued with introductions by H. T. Sheringham. Cape, 1906, 1907, 1908.

SHERINGHAM, H. T. *Coarse Fishing.* Black, 1912.

Out of print but worth much hunting for.

WALKER, RICHARD. *Still-Water Angling.* MacGibbon & Kee, 1953. 18s. Revised edition in preparation.

The 44 lb. carp caught by Mr. Walker and now swimming in a tank in the Aquarium of the Zoological Gardens, Regent's Park has endowed its captor with immortality. In this book Mr. Walker tells other people how to catch huge fish and avoid wasting time on small ones. He describes his carp-fishing, at night, with a fixed spool reel and an electric gadget to warn the fisher when his floating bait has been taken. A book full of ingenuities.

FLY-TYING

Before 1900

"EPHEMERA". *A Handbook of Angling.* 1853.

HALE, Maj. J. H. *How to Tie Salmon Flies*; 1930. Fishing Gazette, 1st edition, 1892.

With dressings for 361 Salmon Flies.

KELSON, J. M. *The Salmon Fly.* 1899.

Long out of print. Historically important.

HALFORD, F. M. *Floating Flies*, 1886, *Dry Fly Fishing in Theory and Practice*, 1889, *Modern Development of the Dry Fly*, 1910.

MCCLELLAND, H. *How to Tie Flies for Trout and Grayling*. Fishing Gazette, 1st edition, 1899; 1947. 7s. 6d.

PRITT, T. E. *Yorkshire* (in the 2nd edition "North Country") *Trout-flies*, 1886.

Hand-tinted pictures of 62 artificial flies, and detailed recipes for making them.

RONALDS, A. *The Flyfisher's Entomology*. 1836.

THEAKSTON, MICHAEL. *British Angling Flies*. Ripon, 1862.

1900—1955

BURRARD, Sir GERALD. *Fly Tying: Principles and Practice* (1st edition 1940). Herbert Jenkins. Revised edition 1951. 9s. 6d.

A very good practical handbook.

DUNNE, J. W. *Sunshine and the Dry Fly*. Black, 1924; 2nd edition, 1950. 8s. 6d.

Not to be missed.

EDMONDS, H. H. and LEE. *Brook and River Trouting*. Young, 1916.

Like Pritt's, a north country book, illustrating in colour thirty-six artificial flies together with the feathers used. This book was published privately in Bradford in 1916 and no one has been able to persuade the surviving author to bring out a new edition.

HARRIS, J. R. *An Angler's Entomology*. Collins, 1952. 25s.

Approaches the subject from the point of view of the fisherman-naturalist, successfully applying his knowledge, illustrating the insects with good coloured photographs besides giving detailed accounts of them and providing a simple key on the "Animal, Vegetable or Mineral?" system that should make it easy for the fisherman to identify a captured insect even if he is seeing it for the first time.

HENN, T. R. *Practical Fly-Tying*. Black, 1950. 10s. 6d.

With Burrard, Woolley and this book beside him, the amateur fly-dresser should be able to resolve his difficulties as fast as they arise.

MOSELEY, MARTIN. *The Dry-Fly Fisherman's Entomology.* Routledge, 1921.

MOTTRAM, J. C. *Fly-fishing. Some new Arts and Mysteries.* The Field.

Full of suggestions of fly-tying experiments.

SKUES, G. E. M. ("Val Conson"). *Silk, Fur and Feather; the Trout-fly Dresser's Year.* Fishing Gazette, 1950. 7s. 6d.

A useful guide, particularly in the collection of materials.

TAVERNER, ERIC. *Fly Tying for Salmon.* Seeley Service, 1947. 8s. 6d.

WALKER, C. F. *Chalk Stream Flies.* Black, 1953. 25s.

Cdr. Walker writes for fishermen who do not tie their own flies, and do not intend to become entomologists, but do want to be able to recognise the flies on which the fish are feeding and the artificial shop-made flies that have been found best to imitate them. As for every fisherman who ties his own flies there must be at least a hundred who use flies professionally tied, his book should find a large and grateful public. The author borrowed his daughter's paint-box and used it well in painting coloured portraits both of the natural insects and of their artificial imitations.

WILLIAMS, A. COURTNEY. *A Dictionary of Trout Flies.* Black, 2nd edition, 1950. 30s.

An invaluable work of reference that will make intelligible to the uninstructed reader the books and articles of writers who refer to natural and artificial flies by names which are often not as familiar to others as to themselves. It is a book that the man who ties his own flies will be continually consulting if he is wise enough to keep it on his table.

WOOLLEY, ROGER. *Modern Trout-Fly Dressing.* Fishing Gazette, 3rd edition, 1950. 8s. 6d.

MISCELLANEOUS

BARRETT, WALTER H. *A Fisherman's Methods and Memories.* Seeley Service, 1953. 12s. 6d.

Instructive reminiscences and accounts of fishing at Blagdon, and in many rivers, Kennet, Wye, Wylye and the Swedish Ems, famous for its big sea trout. He gives the dressings of the celebrated "Shaving Brush", "Daddy Longlegs" and other successful flies.

FEDDEN, ROMILLY. *"Golden Days"*. Introduction by Sir Robert Bruce Lockhart, 1st edition, 1919. Black, 2nd edition, 1949. 7s. 6d.

By an English painter who settled in Brittany and there worked and fished and enjoyed the friendship of the Bretons. A wise and memorable book that makes friends and keeps them.

EASTWOOD, DOROTHEA. *River Diary*. Wingate, 1950, 12s. 6d.

A charming book of fishing, fishermen, flowers and friends in the form of a diary from March to November, a full season in the valley of the Usk.

HARTMAN, ROBERT. *About Fishing*. Methuen, 4th edition, 1947. 12s. 6d.

Combines elementary instruction for the beginner with ripe wisdom to be pondered by all. It deals first with fishing for the instinctive, unsophisticated salmon and later with fishing for the more intelligent and reasoning trout. It includes some good common sense on the tying of flies illustrated with beautiful clarity by the author.

HILLS, J. W. *River Keeper*. Bles, 2nd edition, 1947.

A book about William James Lunn, the Houghton Club keeper, the inventor of Lunn's Particular, the Houghton Ruby and other flies that have been helping fishermen to catch fish on many rivers besides the Test. Here is much of the garnered wisdom of nearly fifty years at Houghton.

My Sporting Life. Allan, 1936.

Wet fly on the Eden, Dry fly and nymph-fishing on Driffield Beck and Test, Greased Line on the Aberdeenshire Dee. A first-rate book that will surely be reprinted.

MCCRAITH, Sir DOUGLAS. *By Dancing Streams*. Witherby, 1952. 12s. 6d.

A pleasant book of memories of fishing on many English rivers —the Dove, the Test and the Wye—as well as in Austria, Belgium and Newfoundland.

27

RANSOME, ARTHUR. *Rod and Line: together with Aksakov on Fishing*. Cape, 1929. 5s.

I do not like putting my own book in this list, but, unless I do so, I should have to omit Aksakov. Forty years ago on a lake in Russia I promised "that I would some day try to share with other English fishermen the very great pleasure I have been given by the first and most delightful of Russian writers on fishing". It would be ridiculous to pretend that I have changed my mind about him.

RENNIE, JOHN. *I Have been Fishing*. Seeley Service, 1949. 15s.

This book, based on and quoting from the diaries of half a century is just what such a scrap-book should be. John Rennie was a naval architect, a champion caster, a skilful painter in oil and water colour, a first rate fly-dresser and a writer who teaches without for a moment being other than delightful to read.

SAWYER FRANK. *Keeper of the Stream*. Black, 1952. 18s.

Frank Sawyer, head keeper of the Officers Fishing Association water at Netheravon, was born in an old mill house on the river and spent his life at the riverside. A born naturalist and observer, who has learnt to say in writing precisely what he means, he has written a delightful book on flies and trout and grayling, friends and enemies, herons, shrews, human beings, moles, and pike, recording much that others have missed and that his have been the first eyes consciously to see.

TAVERNER, ERIC and MOORE, JOHN. *The Angler's Week-end Book*. Seeley Service, 1949. 12s. 6d.

Full of information, practical or quaint, welcome quotations, songs and what not, a great settler of riverside argument, and a good book to find in a fishing hut or within reach of an armchair.

VENABLES, BERNARD. *Fishing*. Batsford, 1953. 16s.

A little of everything; London, Nottingham and Sheffield styles of float-fishing; wet and dry fly-fishing for trout; salmon and sea-trout fishing; fishermen's clubs and John Eastwood's Angler's Co-operative Association with some account of its magnificent fight on behalf of us all against the pollution of streams, rivers, canals and lakes.

VENABLES, BERNARD and MARSHALL, HOWARD. (Editors) *The Angling Times Book*. James Barrie, 1955. 12s. 6d.

This is a first volume of what is planned as an annual publication, a collection of contributions to *The Angling Times* by some thirty Authors, illustrated by very pleasant black and white drawings and photographs.

OLDER BOOKS

BAINBRIDGE, GEORGE C. *The Flyfisher's Guide*, 1816.

FRANCIS, FRANCIS. *A Book of Angling*, 1867.

FALLODON, GREY OF, VISCOUNT. *Fly-Fishing*. Dent, 1899.

KINGSLEY, CHARLES. *Prose Idylls (Chalk Stream Studies)*. Macmillan, 1873.

PENNELL, H. COLMONDELEY. *The Modern Practical Angler*. Routledge. 1870.

RADCLIFFE, WILLIAM. *Fishing from the Earliest Times*. John Murray.

SCROPE, WILLIAM. *Days and Nights of Salmon Fishing in the Tweed*.

STEWART, W. C. *The Practical Angler*: Edinburgh. Black, 1857.

STODDART, THOMAS TOD. *The Angler's Companion to the Rivers and Lochs of Scotland*. 1847.

TURRELL, Dr. W. J. (Editor) *Ancient Angling Authors*. 1910.

A survey of the older writers with many excerpts.

WALTON, IZAAK and COTTON, CHARLES. *The Compleat Angler*. The first part by Izaak Walton, 1653. The second part by Charles Cotton, 1678. (The two parts together with introduction by John Buchan.) Oxford University Press (World's Classics), 1935. 5s.; also available from Dent (Everyman Library), 1953, 6s.; Nelson's Classics, Edinburgh, 4s. and 5s.; Navarre Society, 1953. 12s. 6d. (illustrated).

WEBSTER, DAVID. *The Angler and the Loop-Rod*. Edinburgh, Blackwood. 1885.

Index of Authors

www.ingramcontent.com/pod-product-compliance
Ingram Content Group UK Ltd.
Pitfield, Milton Keynes, MK11 3LW, UK
UKHW020449010325
455719UK00015B/495